The SICK ROSE

O Rose thou art sick.
The invisible worm.
That flies in the night
In the howling storm.

Has found out thy bed
Of crimson joy.
And his dark secret love
Does thy life destroy.

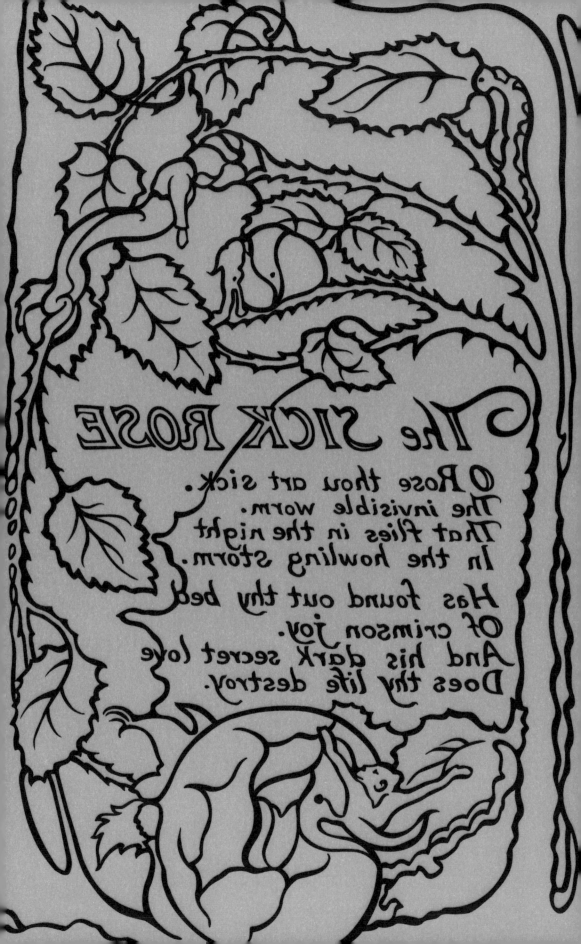

THE FLY

Little Fly
Thy summers play
My thoughtless hand
Has brushed away.

Am not I
A fly like thee?
Or art not thou
A man like me?

For I dance
And drink & sing.
Till some blind hand
Shall brush my wing.

If thought is Life
And strength & breath
And the want
Of thought is death;

Then am I
A happy fly.
If I live
Or if I die.

The Shepherd.

How sweet is the Shepherds sweet lot
From the morn to the evening he strays.
He shall follow his sheep all the day
And his tongue shall be filled with praise.

For he hears the lambs innocent call.
And he hears the ewes tender reply.
He is watchful while they are in peace.
For they know when their Shepherd is nigh.

Infant Joy

I have no name
I am but two days old
What shall I call thee?
I happy am
Joy is my name
Sweet joy befall thee!

Pretty joy!
Sweet joy but two days old.
Sweet joy I call thee:
Thou dost smile
I sing the while
Sweet joy befall thee.

Infant Joy

I have no name
I am but two days old
What shall I call thee?
I happy am
Joy is my name
Sweet joy befall thee!

Pretty joy!
Sweet joy but two days old.
Sweet joy I call thee:
Thou dost smile
I sing the while
Sweet joy befall thee.

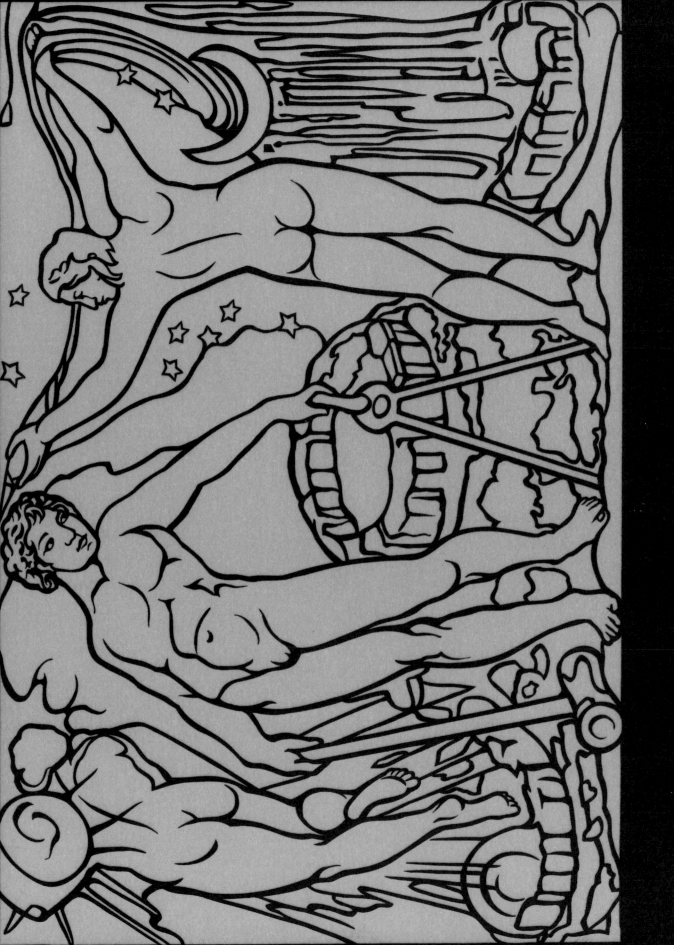

14